The Silver Box

Tony Bradman

Illustrated by Jon Stuart

OXFORD

Hi, I'm Max. These are my friends ...

Cat

Tiger

Ant

This is the story of how I found a silver box. Inside the box was ...

Sorry! You have to read on to find out!

Max was bored. He hated shopping.
He hated it even more when his little
sister needed shoes.

But this was a shopping trip that
would change his life ... forever!

Max and his mum went to a charity shop. They were looking for a book for Molly. That is when he saw it ...

Max was drawn to a far corner of the shop. He loved charity shops. They were full of odd things.

The thing he had spotted was a silver box. It was very sleek and *very* cool.

He had no idea what it was. But he had to have it.

"Oh, no! Not *more* stuff to clutter your bedroom, Max!" said Mum.

Max spent the rest of the morning
trying to get the box open. Was it some
kind of puzzle? Was there a secret code?
In the end, he called his friend, Cat.

Cat and Max met up by the old tree stump in the park. The park was close to Max's house.

"Wow, that *is* cool!" said Cat when she saw the box. But she could not open it.

"If only we knew someone who was good at puzzles," Max said.

"I do," said Cat. "I'll get him!"

Cat ran across to the swings and came back with a shy young boy.

"This is Ant," she said.

"Hi, Ant," said Max. "Could you open this box?"

"Maybe," said Ant. "I'll have a go."

Ant twisted something and pulled something. Then suddenly ...
"WOW!" they all gasped.

"There's a note inside," said Cat. "What does it say?"

Max reached for the piece of paper. He read the note.

Keep us secret.
Keep us safe.

All at once Max felt scared and excited.

Just then, the silver box was snatched from his hand.

"Hey, let *me* have a look!" said a voice.

It was Tiger. He was a boy in Max's class. Tiger pulled out the red watch and put it on. He pushed the buttons.

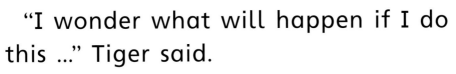

"I wonder what will happen if I do this ..." Tiger said.

"Be careful!" cried Max.

But it was too late. Tiger ... vanished!

"Did you see that?" Cat said, her eyes wide. "Where did he go?"

Max was too shocked to speak. He picked up the box.

"Look! The yellow watch is flashing."

"I can hear a noise," said Ant. "Like somebody calling."

"Yes, but from far away," said Cat.

They all froze. A tiny Tiger was waving at them.

"Look! He's micro-size!" cried Max.

Suddenly, Tiger grew back to full size.

"Now *that* was cool!" said Cat. "How did you do it?"

"I don't know!" said Tiger, grinning. "I just twisted it. Max, why don't you have a try?"

Max looked at the others.

He took a watch. He twisted it. A large X flashed on the screen. He pushed the X and …

The others did the same. They began
to explore a whole new micro-world.
A world where they could have the most
exciting adventures.

Max thought about the note in the silver box. *Keep us secret. Keep us safe.*

"We must look after these watches," he said.

"We can all be micro-friends," said Ant.

"This is going to be great fun!" said Tiger.

So, the micro-friends made a pact. They kept the watches. They kept them secret. They kept them safe.

If only they had known what was in store ...